The Complete Bitcoin Exchange Traded Funds Handbook

Unveiling What You Should Know About This Edge Cutting Potential Investment Product In The World Of Finance

Joel B. Albert
&
U. D. Sudik

I0446805

Why You Should Listen To The Writers

Joel B. Albert —a seasoned cryptocurrency trader and enthusiast, his expertise in cryptocurrency trading extends beyond the theoretical, offering practical insights into the intricate world of digital assets that stem from years of successful trading endeavors.
Joel's perspectives reflect a deep understanding of market dynamics, making him a valuable guide for those seeking to unravel the mysteries of the financial world.

U. D. Sudik, the co-writer, stands as a distinguished figure in the world of Forex trading. With a substantial background coaching a diverse array of Forex traders, from beginners to seasoned professionals, both online and offline, U. D. Sudik possesses a unique ability to distill complex financial concepts into accessible knowledge.

His dedication to sharing insightful and up-to-date information about the financial market through his Telegram channel further underscores his commitment to empowering the trading community.

Together, Joel B. Albert and U. D. Sudik combines their wealth of experience to offer readers a comprehensive and insightful exploration of Bitcoin & Bitcoin Exchange-Traded Funds. Their diverse backgrounds in cryptocurrency and Forex trading create a dynamic synergy, providing readers with a well-rounded perspective that is both practical and informed. Listening to these writers is not just an opportunity to gain knowledge; it's an investment in expertise that can shape your understanding of the financial landscape.

Table Of Contents

INTRODUCTION
Chapter 1
Overview Of The Bitcoin Exchange Traded Funds
  Brief History of Bitcoin ETFs
  What are Bitcoin ETFs?
  Types Of Bitcoin ETFs
Chapter 2
Bitcoin and Blockchain Basics
  Overview of Bitcoin
  Blockchain Technology Fundamentals
  Significance of Cryptocurrency in the Financial Market
Chapter 3
The Evolution of Cryptocurrency Investments
  Historical Context of Cryptocurrency Investing
  Role of ETFs in Traditional and Crypto Market
    Traditional Market:
    Cryptocurrency Market:
Chapter 4
The Need for Bitcoin ETFs
  Market Demand and Trends in Cryptocurrency Investments
  Advantages of Exchange Traded Funds(ETFs)
Chapter 4
How Bitcoin ETF Works
  Tracking Bitcoin's Performance
  Creation and Redemption Process in Bitcoin ETFs

Chapter 5

Risks and Challenges in BTCETFs Investing

    Market Volatility and Risk Reduction

    Regulatory Considerations in BTCETFs Investing

Chapter 6

Investing in BTCETFs (A Step-by-Step Guide):

    How to Invest In Bitcoin ETFs

    Buying and Selling Process of BTCETFs

        Buying BTCETFs:

        Selling BTCETFs:

    How to Choosing the Right BTCETFs

Chapter 7

Comparing BTCETFs with Traditional Investments

    Key Differences and Similarities with Traditional ETFs

        Differences:

        Similarities:

    Market Impact and Investor Sentiment

        Market Impact:

        Investor Sentiment:

Chapter 8

Case Studies and Performance Analysis

    Examining Historical Data of U.S Approved BTCETFs

    Real-world Examples of BTCETFs and Total Assets

Chapter 9

The Future Outlook and Emerging Trends

    Future Predictions for BTCETFs

Future Predictions for Bitcoin/BTCETFs Spot after SEC's Approval

Chapter 10

FAQs and Glossary.

Frequently Asked Questions And Answers

Glossary of key terms in Cryptocurrency and ETFs financial market.

Cryptocurrency Glossary:

ETFs Glossary:

Recap of Key Takeaways

CONCLUSION

INTRODUCTION

Welcome to the comprehensive exploration of "Bitcoin Exchange-Traded Funds – Bridging Worlds of Finance." In the ever-evolving landscape of cryptocurrency and traditional finance, the emergence of Bitcoin ETFs marks a pivotal moment that captures the attention of investors, enthusiasts, and financial experts alike.

This journey delves into the intricacies of BTC-ETFs, unraveling their significance, regulatory challenges, the distinct types that pave the way for investors to gain exposure to the dynamic world of Bitcoin, etc.

From the early proposals by visionaries like the Winklevoss twins to the historic approval in 2021, each step in the evolution of Bitcoin ETFs is dissected to provide a comprehensive understanding of their role in shaping the financial future.

As we navigate the basics of ETFs distinguishing between Spot and Futures Bitcoin ETFs, and exploring the regulatory considerations that have shaped their narrative, this book aims to equip readers with the knowledge needed to engage confidently in the cryptocurrency market.

The discussions within this financial Bible extend beyond the technicalities, delving into expert predictions, future outlooks, and crucial advice for investors.
Whether you are a seasoned investor, a newcomer, or a curious enthusiast, this book serves as a compass, guiding you through the intricacies of BTC-ETFs and empowering you to make educated decisions in the volatile world of digital assets.

So, you're about to embark on a financial educational journey with us as we unravel the mysteries, explore the potential, and navigate the intricate tapestry of Bitcoin, Bitcoin Exchange-Traded Funds, and other crucial factors in the world of finance, offering you clarity in a rapidly evolving financial landscape.

Let the pages of this eye-opening guide be your gateway to a deeper understanding of this transformative chapter in the realms of finance.

Chapter 1

Overview Of The Bitcoin Exchange Traded Funds

Brief History of Bitcoin ETFs

The emergence of Bitcoin Exchange Traded Funds (ETFs) represents a significant chapter in the evolution of cryptocurrency and traditional finance convergence. The process toward creating a Bitcoin ETF began in 2013, when the Winklevoss twins submitted the initial proposal for a Bitcoin ETF to the US Securities and Exchange Commission (SEC).

However, regulatory concerns and uncertainties surrounding the cryptocurrency market delayed the approval process. It wasn't until October 2021 that the SEC finally granted approval (only to Futures BTC ETFs) for the ProShares Bitcoin Strategy ETF and the Valkyrie Bitcoin Strategy ETF. This marked a groundbreaking moment as these ETFs became the first of their kind to be listed on major U.S. stock exchanges.

The delays in approving Bitcoin ETFs were primarily rooted in concerns related to market manipulation, liquidity, and investor protection. Regulatory authorities sought to strike a balance between fostering innovation in the burgeoning cryptocurrency space and ensuring adequate safeguards for investors.

The approval of the ProShares Bitcoin Strategy ETF(Futures only), trading under the ticker BITO, paved the way for institutional and retail investors to gain exposure to Bitcoin through a regulated investment vehicle. The ETF, designed to track Bitcoin futures contracts, aimed to provide a more accessible entry point for traditional investors who were keen on participating in the cryptocurrency market.

The green light for Bitcoin ETFs in the U.S. signaled a shift in perception and acceptance of digital assets within mainstream financial markets as the cryptocurrency landscape continues to evolve.

Keynote:

In the U.S, the approval of Bitcoin Exchange Traded Funds (ETFs) marks a significant milestone in the convergence of cryptocurrency and traditional finance.

Despite regulatory hurdles dating back to 2013, this approval signals a transformative shift, offering both institutional and retail investors a regulated entry point into the cryptocurrency market. The acceptance of Bitcoin ETFs reflects the evolving landscape of digital assets within mainstream financial markets.

What are Bitcoin ETFs?

Bitcoin exchange-traded funds(BTC-ETFs) are financial products that allow investors to gain exposure to the price movements of bitcoin without actually holding the asset itself. ETFs can be bought, sold and traded on traditional stock market exchanges instead of cryptocurrency trading platforms, making it easier for traditional investors to participate in the cryptocurrency market. BTC-ETF is a solid way to give mainstream investors and speculators bitcoin price exposure through a reliable vehicle with which they are likely already familiar.

Exchange-traded funds are not a new concept and are widely used in the financial sector. ETFs can be found to gain price exposure to different assets and industries, including commodities and currencies, or can be set up to focus on companies that are environmentally friendly or focus on diversity.

Types Of Bitcoin ETFs

There are only two main types of bitcoin ETFs: Spot and Futures Bitcoin ETFs.

Spot Bitcoin ETF: A bitcoin spot ETF is a type of exchange-traded fund or an investment vehicle that aims to provide investors with direct exposure to the current or actual market price of bitcoin in their regular brokerage accounts. Spot in this context refers to the immediate or current price of the underlying asset, which is bitcoin itself. A bitcoin spot ETF typically holds genuine bitcoin as its underlying asset and aims to closely track the real-time price of bitcoin.

Futures Bitcoin ETFs: Futures ETFs do not hold actual bitcoin. Instead, they use bitcoin futures contracts to gain exposure to the cryptocurrency. A bitcoin futures contract allows investors to speculate and wager on the asset's future price. Futures bitcoin ETFs may perform differently from spot bitcoin ETFs, and expenses associated with rolling over or settling futures contracts may exist. Some bitcoin futures

ETFs are designed to give leveraged or inverse exposure to the price of bitcoin, allowing investors to amplify both profits and losses.

Keynote:

Bitcoin Exchange-Traded Funds (BTC-ETFs) provide a convenient way for mainstream investors to access bitcoin's price movements without holding the cryptocurrency directly. Tradable on traditional stock exchanges, BTC-ETFs offer familiarity and ease of participation. They come in two main types: Spot, holding actual bitcoin for real-time price tracking, and Futures, using contracts for exposure, with potential for leveraged or inverse impact. Understanding these distinctions is key, especially regarding costs associated with futures contracts.

Chapter 2

Bitcoin and Blockchain Basics

Overview of Bitcoin

Bitcoin, often referred to as digital gold, is a decentralized digital currency that marked the inception of blockchain technology and cryptocurrency. It was introduced in a 2008 whitepaper titled "Bitcoin: A Peer-to-Peer Electronic Cash System" by an individual or group under the pseudonym Satoshi Nakamoto.

At its core, Bitcoin operates on a peer-to-peer network, eliminating the need for intermediaries such as banks. It's built on a blockchain, a distributed ledger that records all transactions across a network of computers. This decentralized nature provides transaction history transparency, security, and immutability.

The total supply of Bitcoin is capped at 21 million, a deliberate design choice to emulate scarcity and prevent inflation. This scarcity is maintained through a process called mining, where participants, known as miners, use computational power to solve complex mathematical problems and validate transactions. These miners are then rewarded with newly created bitcoins in return.

Bitcoin transactions are pseudonymous; each user is represented by a cryptographic address rather than personal information. The use of public and private keys ensures secure ownership and transfer of bitcoins.

One of Bitcoin's groundbreaking features is its consensus algorithm, Proof of Work (PoW), which ensures agreement on the state of the blockchain. This process involves miners competing to solve mathematical puzzles, adding a new block to the chain approximately every ten minutes.

The price of Bitcoin is determined by market demand and supply dynamics, and it has gained attention as a store of value, a hedge against inflation, and a decentralized alternative to traditional currencies.

Keynote:

Despite its success, Bitcoin has faced criticisms, including concerns about energy consumption due to mining activities and its potential use in illegal transactions. Nevertheless, it remains a pioneering force in the world of cryptocurrencies, paving the way for various blockchain applications and innovations. Understanding Bitcoin is foundational to exploring the broader landscape of blockchain technology and its transformative impact on finance and beyond.

Blockchain Technology Fundamentals

Blockchain technology, the underlying innovation behind cryptocurrencies like Bitcoin, Ethereum, Tron, etc, –is a decentralized and distributed ledger system that has the potential to revolutionize various industries.

Here are the key fundamentals of blockchain:

1. Decentralization:
* Blockchain is based on a network of computers called nodes that collaborate to validate and record transactions.
* No central authority governs the entire system, reducing the risk of a single point of failure.

2. Distributed Ledger:
* The ledger, or record of transactions, is distributed across all participants in the network.
* Each participant has a copy of the entire blockchain, ensuring transparency and redundancy.

3. Immutable Record:
* Once a transaction block is put to the blockchain, it is almost hard to change or delete it.
* Immutability is achieved through cryptographic hash functions that link each block to the previous one.

4. Consensus Mechanisms:
* Consensus algorithms guarantee that all nodes agree on the blockchain's current state.
* Examples include Proof of Work (used in Bitcoin) and Proof of Stake(used in Ethereum), which validate transactions and secure the network.

5. Smart Contracts:
* Self-executing contracts with coded terms written directly into the blockchain.
* Automate and enforce contractual agreement execution, removing the need for middlemen.

6. Cryptographic Security:

* Public and private key cryptography secures transactions and provides ownership of digital assets.
* Private keys are kept secret, while public keys are shared to facilitate secure transactions.

7. Transparent and Auditable:
* All transactions are visible to participants in the blockchain network.
* Transparency enhances accountability, and the entire transaction history can be audited.

8. Tokenization:
* Digital assets or tokens can represent real-world assets like real estate or stocks.
* Tokenization enables fractional ownership and facilitates faster, more efficient transactions.

9. Interoperability:
* Blockchain platforms aim to interoperate seamlessly with each other.
* Standards like Interledger Protocol (ILP) and others facilitate cross-blockchain transactions.

10. Permissioned vs. Permissionless Blockchains:
* Permissionless blockchains, such as Bitcoin and Ethereum, enable anybody to join the network.
* Permissioned blockchains restrict access, often used in enterprise settings.

Keynote:

Understanding these fundamentals provides a solid foundation for grasping the potential of blockchain technology beyond cryptocurrencies. As blockchain continues to evolve, its applications are expanding into supply chain management, healthcare, finance, and many other sectors, promising increased efficiency, security, and transparency.

Significance of Cryptocurrency in the Financial Market

Since the introduction of Cryptocurrency like Bitcoin in 2009, it has progressively become a transformative force in the financial market, influencing various aspects of traditional finance.

Here are key points highlighting the significance of cryptocurrencies:

1. Decentralization and Financial Inclusion:
* Cryptocurrencies operate on decentralized networks, providing financial access to individuals without relying on traditional banking systems.
* Particularly significant in areas with limited access to banking or financial services.

2. Global Accessibility:
* Cryptocurrencies enable instant and borderless transactions, reducing the need for intermediaries like banks and facilitating cross-border payments.
* Access to the financial market is extended globally without traditional barriers.

3. Transaction Costs:
* Cryptocurrency transactions often have lower fees(known as network fee or gas fee) compared to traditional financial services.
* This can make microtransactions and international transfers more cost-effective.

4. Blockchain Tech. and Security:
* The underlying blockchain technology ensures the security and integrity of transactions.
* Immutable ledgers and cryptographic techniques enhance trust and transparency.

5. Store of Value and Hedging Against Inflation:
* Cryptocurrencies like Bitcoin are considered digital assets and as a store of value.
* Some investors in today's world use cryptocurrencies as a hedge against inflation and economic uncertainties.

6. Innovation in Financial Services:
* Cryptocurrencies have spurred innovation in financial services, leading to the

development of decentralized finance (DeFi) platforms.
* DeFi offers a range of financial services without traditional intermediaries.

7. Tokenization of Assets:
* Cryptocurrencies facilitate the tokenization of real-world assets, allowing fractional ownership of high-value assets like real estate or artworks —Nonfungible tokens(NFTs).
* This enhances liquidity and accessibility.

8. Initial Coin Offerings (ICOs) and Token Sales:
* Cryptocurrencies have introduced new fundraising models like ICOs, allowing projects to raise capital directly from the community.
* Token sales have become a means of financing blockchain-based ventures.

9. Increased Financial Privacy:
* Certain cryptocurrencies, like Monero and Zcash, prioritize privacy features.

* Users can conduct transactions with a higher degree of anonymity compared to traditional financial transactions.

10. Market Diversification:
* The presence of cryptocurrencies adds a new asset class to investment portfolios, offering diversification opportunities for investors.
* Central banks and financial institutions are exploring digital currencies in response to market diversification.

Keynote:

As the cryptocurrency market continues to mature, its impact on the financial landscape is likely to grow, challenging existing norms and fostering increased innovation in the broader financial industry.

Chapter 3

The Evolution of Cryptocurrency Investments

Historical Context of Cryptocurrency Investing

The historical context of cryptocurrency investing is a major journey in the financial world marked by innovation, volatility, and a transformative shift in the financial landscape.

Here are key points that illustrate the evolution of cryptocurrency investments:

1. Genesis of Bitcoin (2009):
* Cryptocurrency investing began with the creation of Bitcoin in 2009 by the pseudonymous Satoshi Nakamoto.
* Bitcoin's whitepaper introduced the concept of a decentralized, peer-to-peer

digital currency, setting the stage for a new era of financial possibilities.

2. Early Adopters and Enthusiasts (2010-2013):
* The first few years saw a community of early adopters and enthusiasts exploring the potential of Bitcoin.
* Bitcoin's value grew from virtually nothing to a few cents(gradually growing up) attracting attention and curiosity.

3. Market Expansion and Altcoins (2014-2016):
* The cryptocurrency market expanded with the introduction of alternative coins (altcoins) beyond Bitcoin, such as Litecoin, and Ripple.
* Altcoins brought new functionalities and use cases, diversifying the investment landscape.

4. ICO Boom and Regulatory Scrutiny (2017):
* The Initial Coin Offering (ICO) boom emerged, enabling projects to raise funds through token sales.

* Regulatory scrutiny increased as the ICO space faced challenges related to fraud and investor protection.

5. Bitcoin's Meteoric Rise (2017-2018):
* Bitcoin experienced a historic price surge in late 2017, reaching an all-time high(Open–$966, High–$19,892).
* Institutional interest grew, but the market also witnessed a subsequent correction in 2018.

6. Institutional Involvement and Maturation (2019):
* Institutional players entered the space with the launch of Bitcoin futures and investment products.
* Regulatory frameworks began to take shape, contributing to a more mature and regulated environment.

7. DeFi and NFTs (2020):
* The rise of Decentralized Finance (DeFi) platforms introduced new ways to earn and lend in the crypto space.
* Non-Fungible Tokens (NFTs) gained prominence, representing unique digital

assets and creating a new avenue for investment.

8. Integration with Traditional Finance (Ongoing):
* Cryptocurrency investments are increasingly integrated into traditional financial systems.
* Adoption of blockchain technology by established companies and financial institutions further legitimizes the industry.

Keynote:

Understanding the historical context of cryptocurrency investing provides insights into the industry's resilience, adaptability, and its ongoing evolution as a dynamic and impactful component of the broader financial landscape.

Watch Out For Our New Release: The History Of Cryptocurrency– Price Trend Of Bitcoin.

Role of ETFs in Traditional and Crypto Market

Exchange-Traded Funds (ETFs) play a crucial role in both traditional and cryptocurrency markets, offering unique advantages and opportunities.

Here's an overview of their roles in each:

Traditional Market:

1. Diversification:
* ETFs provide investors with exposure to a diversified portfolio of assets, reducing individual asset risk.
* They cover various sectors, industries, and asset classes, allowing investors to achieve broad market exposure.

2. Liquidity and Trading Efficiency:
* ETFs, like individual stocks, trade on stock exchanges, giving investors intraday liquidity.
* Market makers help maintain liquidity by facilitating the buying and selling of ETF shares.

3. Cost-Effective Investing:
* ETFs frequently have lower expense ratios than mutual funds, making them a more cost-effective investing alternative.
* Passive ETFs, which track an index, have lower management fees compared to actively managed funds.

4. Accessibility:
* ETFs make it easy for retail investors to access markets that might be challenging to enter directly.
* They provide a straightforward way to invest in specific sectors, commodities, or regions.

5. Transparency:
* ETFs disclose their holdings regularly, providing transparency to investors about the assets in the fund.
* This transparency helps investors make informed decisions based on the fund's composition.

Cryptocurrency Market:

1. Mainstream Adoption:
* Cryptocurrency ETFs bridge the gap between traditional finance and the digital asset space, making it easier for traditional investors to gain exposure to cryptocurrencies.
* They provide a familiar investment vehicle within the regulated framework of traditional financial markets.

2. Risk Mitigation:
* Cryptocurrency ETFs can mitigate some of the risks associated with direct cryptocurrency investments, such as security concerns and custody issues.
* They offer a more regulated and secure way for investors to participate in the crypto market.

3. Market Integration:
* Cryptocurrency ETFs contribute to the integration of digital assets into the broader financial ecosystem.
* Institutional investors, who may be restricted from directly holding

cryptocurrencies, can invest indirectly through regulated ETFs.

4. Simplified Investment Process:
* Cryptocurrency ETFs simplify the investment process for those unfamiliar with the complexities of managing private keys and wallets.
* Investors can buy and sell shares of the ETF through traditional brokerage accounts.

5. Price Discovery:
* Cryptocurrency ETFs can contribute to price discovery by reflecting the market sentiment and demand for digital assets within the traditional financial infrastructure.

Keynote:

Understanding the role of ETFs in both traditional and cryptocurrency markets highlights their versatility and significance in providing investors with diversified, cost-effective, and regulated exposure to various asset classes.

Chapter 4

The Need for Bitcoin ETFs

Market Demand and Trends in Cryptocurrency Investments

The need for Bitcoin Exchange Traded Funds (ETFs) stems from a dynamic interplay of market demand and evolving trends in cryptocurrency investments.
Here is an exploration of these factors:

1. Growing Investor Interest:
* The cryptocurrency market has witnessed a surge in investor interest, ranging from individual retail investors to institutional players.
* Bitcoin, as a leading digital asset, has become a focal point for those seeking exposure to the potential returns offered by the crypto space.

2. Institutional Participation:
* Institutional adoption of cryptocurrencies has gained momentum, with major financial institutions acknowledging the value of digital assets.
* Bitcoin ETFs can provide a regulated and familiar investment avenue for institutional investors to allocate funds to the crypto market.

3. Risk Mitigation and Diversification:
* Investors recognize the need for risk mitigation strategies in the volatile cryptocurrency market.
* Bitcoin ETFs offer a regulated and diversified approach, allowing investors to gain exposure to Bitcoin without directly(involving in the risk of) holding the underlying asset.

4. Accessible Entry Points:
* Cryptocurrency exchanges, while popular, can be perceived as complex by some investors.
* Bitcoin ETFs simplify the investment process, providing a familiar structure for

buying and selling shares on traditional stock exchanges.

5. Market Maturity and Regulation:
* As the cryptocurrency market matures, regulatory frameworks are gradually taking shape.
* Bitcoin ETFs operate within established regulatory guidelines, contributing to the legitimacy and acceptance of digital assets in traditional finance.

6. Economic Uncertainties and Inflation Hedging:
* Economic uncertainties and concerns about traditional fiat currencies losing value have driven interest in alternative assets.
* Bitcoin, often referred to as "digital gold or digital asset," is viewed as a potential hedge against inflation, attracting investors seeking a store of value.

7. Global Economic Trends:
* Cryptocurrencies, including Bitcoin, Ethereum, etc, are increasingly recognized as part of a diversified investment strategy.

* Global economic trends, such as the rise of digital payments(Cashless Policies) and blockchain integration, further fuel the demand for exposure to digital assets.

8. Retail Investor Participation:
* Retail investors, drawn by the allure of potential gains, contribute to the demand for accessible investment options.
* Bitcoin ETFs cater to this demand by offering a straightforward entry point for retail investors looking to participate in the crypto market.

9. Technology and Innovation:
* Ongoing technological advancements in the blockchain and cryptocurrency space drive innovation.
* Bitcoin ETFs represent a financial innovation that aligns with the evolving technological landscape, providing investors with modern investment tools.

Keynote:

The need for Bitcoin ETFs is intricately linked to the evolving dynamics of market demand, investor preferences, and the maturation of the cryptocurrency ecosystem. These ETFs serve as a bridge between traditional finance and the burgeoning digital asset space, meeting the diverse investment needs of a broad range of market participants.

Advantages of Exchange Traded Funds(ETFs)

Exchange-Traded Funds (ETFs) offer a range of advantages that contribute to their popularity and widespread use linked with new traders and investors in the general financial market.

Here are key benefits associated with ETFs:

1. Diversification: ETFs hold a diversified portfolio of assets, spreading risk across multiple securities.

- Benefit: New investors can achieve broad market exposure with a single investment, reducing the impact of individual stock volatility.

2. Liquidity: ETFs trade on stock exchanges like individual stocks, providing high liquidity.

- Benefit: New investors can easily buy or sell shares at market prices during trading hours, ensuring efficient transactions.

3. Cost Efficiency: ETFs typically have lower expense ratios compared to actively managed mutual funds.

- Benefit: Cost-effective investment options allow new investors to allocate more of their capital to the market without incurring high fees.

4. Accessibility: ETFs can be bought and sold through brokerage accounts, making them accessible to individual investors.

- Benefit: New investors can participate in various markets and sectors without the need for a substantial initial investment.

5. Transparency: ETFs disclose their holdings daily, providing transparency about the fund's composition.

- Benefit: New investors can make informed decisions by understanding what assets the ETF holds, enhancing overall transparency.

6. Flexibility: ETFs cover diverse asset classes, allowing investors to tailor their portfolios to specific investment objectives.

- Benefit: New investors can choose ETFs aligned with their risk tolerance and investment preferences.

7. Intraday Trading: ETFs can be traded throughout the trading day at market prices.
- Benefit: New investors can react promptly to market developments, adjusting their positions as needed within the same trading day.

8. Risk Mitigation: Inverse ETFs and other specialized ETFs can help investors hedge against market downturns.
- Benefit: New investors can use ETFs to manage risk and potentially offset losses during market corrections.

9. Professional Management: Actively managed ETFs are overseen by experienced fund managers.
- Benefit: New investors can benefit from professional management strategies without needing to actively manage their portfolios.

10. Educational Resources: Many ETF providers offer educational materials and resources for investors.

- Benefit: New investors can access information and insights, aiding in their understanding of investment principles and market dynamics.

Keynote:

Exchange Traded Funds (ETFs) offer new investors and traders a cost-effective, transparent, and flexible entry into the financial markets. With diversified portfolios, easy accessibility, and intraday trading options, ETFs empower investors to navigate markets efficiently. Their transparency, low costs, and educational resources make them a valuable tool for building diversified portfolios while managing risk. Overall, ETFs provide a solid foundation for new investors to start their journey in the world of investing and trading.

Chapter 4

How Bitcoin ETF Works

Tracking Bitcoin's Performance

Bitcoin Exchange Traded Funds (BTCETFs) employ a unique mechanism to track and replicate the performance of Bitcoin. Understanding how Bitcoin ETFs track the digital asset's performance is crucial for investors looking to gain exposure to the cryptocurrency market.

Here is an overview of the process:

1. Index-Based Tracking:
* Bitcoin ETFs often utilize an index as a benchmark, typically the performance of Bitcoin itself or a custom-designed index reflecting the cryptocurrency market.

2. Futures Contracts:

* Some Bitcoin ETFs may invest in Bitcoin futures contracts rather than holding the physical asset.
* Futures contracts enable ETFs to track the price movements of Bitcoin without directly owning the cryptocurrency.

3. Synthetic Replication:
* In certain cases, ETFs may use financial derivatives and other instruments to synthetically replicate the performance of Bitcoin.
* This approach allows for flexibility in the fund's structure and can enhance liquidity.

4. Price Monitoring and Adjustments:
* Continuous monitoring of Bitcoin's price is integral to ETFs tracking its live performance.
* ETF managers regularly adjust the portfolio to ensure alignment with the chosen benchmark or index.

5. Net Asset Value (NAV) Calculation:
* The Net Asset Value of the ETF is calculated regularly based on the current market value of the Bitcoin holdings.

* This NAV reflects the per-share value of the ETF and is crucial for pricing and trading activities.

6. Dividend Handling (when applicable):
* Some Bitcoin ETFs may distribute income generated from activities like lending Bitcoin or earning interest on holdings.
* Dividends, when applicable, are typically reinvested or distributed to shareholders.

Keynotes:

Understanding the meticulous process of tracking Bitcoin's performance in ETFs is fundamental for investors seeking exposure to the cryptocurrency market. This methodical approach, involving various financial instruments and market mechanisms, aims to provide a reliable and regulated means for investors to participate in the potential returns and risks associated with the underlying asset(Bitcoin).

Creation and Redemption Process in Bitcoin ETFs

The creation and redemption process is a fundamental mechanism in the operation of Bitcoin Exchange Traded Funds (BTCETFs), facilitating the seamless flow of shares in response to market demand.

Here is an in-depth explanation of how this process works:

1. Authorized Participants (APs):
* ETFs enlist specialized entities known as Authorized Participants (APs).
* These APs are typically large financial institutions or market makers with the authority to create and redeem ETF shares.

2. Creation of New Shares:
* When there is investor demand for ETFs(BTCETFs) shares, APs can create new shares.
* APs can deliver a specified amount of Bitcoin or its equivalent value to the ETF issuer in exchange for newly created ETF shares.

3. Delivery of Bitcoin:
* In the creation process, APs may transfer actual Bitcoin or cash (in some cases) to the ETF issuer.
* The amount is proportionate to the number of ETF shares being created.

4. In-Kind Transactions:
* Creation typically occurs through in-kind transactions, where the APs can contribute actual assets(Bitcoin) to the ETF's holdings.
* This mechanism helps the ETF maintain its correlation with the underlying asset (Bitcoin) and enhances liquidity.

5. Creation Basket and NAV Calculation:
* The basket of assets delivered by APs during creation is often referred to as the "creation basket."
* The Net Asset Value (NAV) of the ETF is calculated based on this creation basket, reflecting the per-share value of the fund.

6. Redemption of Shares:
* Conversely, when investors want to redeem their ETF shares, APs can facilitate the process.

* APs deliver ETF shares to the issuer in exchange for the underlying assets in the form of Bitcoin(for this context).

7. Arbitrage Opportunities:
* The creation and redemption process creates arbitrage opportunities in the market.
* If the ETF's market price deviates from its NAV, arbitrageurs can step in, either creating or redeeming shares to capitalize on the price differential.

8. Market Efficiency and Price Alignment:
* The continuous creation and redemption process helps maintain the ETF's market price in close alignment with its NAV.
* This mechanism contributes to market efficiency and ensures that the ETF accurately reflects the performance of the underlying asset(Bitcoin).

Keynote:

Understanding the ETF creation and redemption process provides insight into the mechanisms that enable the efficient functioning of Bitcoin ETFs. This process not only ensures liquidity but also helps maintain the ETF's performance closely tied to the underlying asset(Bitcoin) market, enhancing the overall integrity of the investment vehicle.

Chapter 5

Risks and Challenges in BTCETFs Investing

Market Volatility and Risk Reduction

Investing in Bitcoin Exchange Traded Funds (BTCETFs) comes with inherent risks, and managing market volatility is a crucial aspect for you as an investor seeking to navigate the cryptocurrency landscape. Here is an exploration of market volatility and strategies for risk reduction in BTCETFs investing:

1. Volatility in Cryptocurrency Markets:
* Cryptocurrency markets, including Bitcoin, are known for their price volatility.

* Rapid and substantial price fluctuations can pose challenges for investors, impacting the value of BTCETFs.

2. Risk Reduction Through Diversification:
* Diversifying investments across different assets within the BTCETFs can help mitigate the impact of volatility.
* Including a mix of cryptocurrencies and possibly other asset classes can enhance portfolio resilience.

3. Active Management Strategies:
* Some BTCETFs employ active management strategies to navigate market volatility.
* Skilled fund managers may adjust the ETF's holdings based on market conditions to optimize risk-adjusted returns.

4. Hedging Techniques:
* BTCETFs managers may utilize hedging techniques to offset potential losses during periods of high volatility.
* Derivative instruments or options contracts can be employed strategically to manage downside risk.

5. Stress Testing Portfolios:
* Conducting stress tests on the BTCETFs portfolio helps assess how it may perform under extreme market conditions.
* This proactive approach allows for adjustments to the portfolio composition to enhance resilience.

6. Setting Risk Tolerance:
* Investors should define their risk tolerance and investment goals before entering the BTCETFs market.
* Understanding the level of risk you're willing to undertake is crucial for making informed investment decisions.

7. Regular Portfolio Rebalancing:
* Periodic rebalancing of the BTCETFs portfolio ensures that it aligns with the investor's risk profile and market conditions.
* This disciplined approach helps manage exposure to excessive risk.

8. Monitoring Regulatory Developments:

* Regulatory changes can impact the cryptocurrency market and, consequently, BTCETFs.

* Regular monitoring of regulatory developments can help you(investors) stay informed about potential shifts in market dynamics.

9. Educational Awareness:

* Investors should be educated about the nature of cryptocurrency markets and the associated risks.

* Informed investors are better equipped to make decisions during periods of heightened volatility.

10. Using Stop-Loss Orders:

* Implementing stop-loss orders(if applicable) allows investors to set predetermined exit points to limit potential losses.

* This risk management tool automates the selling of assets if prices fall below a specified threshold.

Keynote:

While market volatility is an inherent aspect of BTCETFs investing, strategic risk reduction measures empower investors to navigate challenges effectively. By combining diversification, active management, and risk-aware strategies, investors can position themselves to potentially capitalize on opportunities while managing the impact of market fluctuations.

Regulatory Considerations in BTCETFs Investing

Investing in Bitcoin Exchange Traded Funds (BTCETFs) is subject to various risks, and navigating regulatory considerations is a crucial aspect for investors aiming to participate in the cryptocurrency market through ETFs.

Here is an exploration of the regulatory landscape and key considerations for BTCETFs investing:

1. Evolution of Regulatory Frameworks:

* Cryptocurrency markets, including Bitcoin, are evolving, and regulatory frameworks are in a state of development.
* Investors should stay informed about the changing regulatory landscape and potential impacts on BTCETFs.

2. Approval and Listing:

* BTCETFs must undergo regulatory approval processes before being listed on exchanges.

* Investors should verify the regulatory status and approval of BTCETFs to ensure compliance with relevant authorities.

3. SEC Scrutiny in the U.S:
* In the United States, the Securities and Exchange Commission (SEC) plays a key role in regulating investment products, including ETFs.
* SEC scrutiny and decisions regarding BTCETFs applications can significantly influence their availability to investors.

4. Global Regulatory Variances:
* Regulatory approaches to cryptocurrency ETFs vary globally.
* Investors with an international focus should be aware of regulatory variances in different jurisdictions that may impact BTCETFs.

5. Risk of Regulatory Changes:
* Regulatory changes, such as the introduction of new laws or amendments, can impact the cryptocurrency market linked with its ETFs.

* Investors should anticipate and assess the potential effects of regulatory shifts on BTCETFs.

6. Market Surveillance and Manipulation:
* Regulators aim to ensure fair and transparent markets by implementing surveillance measures.
* Investors should consider the effectiveness of market surveillance mechanisms in detecting and preventing market manipulation.

7. Custody and Security Standards:
* Regulatory standards for custody and security of digital assets held by BTCETFs are crucial for investor protection.
* Investors should assess the adherence of BTCETFs to establish custody and security protocols.

8. AML/KYC Compliance:
* Anti-Money Laundering (AML) and Know Your Customer (KYC) compliance are essential regulatory requirements.
* Investors should choose BTCETFs that prioritize robust AML/KYC measures to

mitigate the risk of illicit or fraudulent activities.

9. Liquidity and Market Integrity:
* Regulatory oversight aims to maintain liquidity and market integrity.
* Investors should evaluate how regulatory measures contribute to the liquidity and overall integrity of BTCETFs.

Keynote:

Regulatory considerations play a pivotal role in BTCETFs investing. Investors should remain vigilant about regulatory developments, assess compliance with established standards, and understand how regulatory dynamics may influence the performance and availability of BTCETFs in the market(While the SEC has approved BTCETFs Futures, the spot is under review and yet to be approved as at the time of writing this book).

Chapter 6

Investing in BTCETFs (A Step-by-Step Guide):

How to Invest In Bitcoin ETFs

Initiating an investment in a Bitcoin ETF entails a sequential process, commencing with the establishment of a brokerage account. In today's expansive online brokerage landscape, investors can choose from a variety of platforms to initiate this foundational step.

Once the investor has successfully set up their brokerage account, the acquisition of Bitcoin ETFs follows a streamlined procedure akin to purchasing conventional stocks or other exchange-traded funds (ETFs). This involves navigating the brokerage interface, where the investor can effortlessly locate the Bitcoin ETF of interest by searching for its designated ticker symbol. Subsequently, they can input the desired quantity of shares they wish to acquire and execute the purchase with a simple click.

It is imperative to note that, in contrast to traditional stocks, ETFs incur an annual expense ratio. This fee is automatically deducted from the investor's account, constituting a crucial aspect of the overall cost associated with holding and managing the Bitcoin ETF investment. As investors traverse the realm of ETFs, this consideration underscores the importance of evaluating expense ratios to gauge the ongoing costs associated with maintaining the investment over time.

Keynote:

Investors should bear in mind that cryptocurrencies, including Bitcoin, constitute a relatively new and volatile asset class(which in turn affect its ETFs). It is prudent not to invest more than one(you) can afford to lose. Seeking advice from a financial advisor before making any investment decisions is always a recommended and wise approach.

Buying and Selling Process of BTCETFs

The process of buying and selling Bitcoin Exchange Traded Funds (BTCETFs) involves a series of steps that investors can navigate through online brokerage platforms.

Here is a comprehensive overview of the buying and selling process:

Buying BTCETFs:

1. Open a Brokerage Account: The initial step is to open a brokerage account. You(Investors) have a plethora of online brokerage options available, and choosing a reputable platform is crucial(earlier stated).

2. Fund Your Account: Once the account is set up, you(investors) need to fund it. This involves depositing funds into the brokerage account, which will be used to purchase BTCETFs shares.

3. Research and Select BTCETFs: Before making a purchase, you(investors) should conduct thorough research on available BTCETFs. Considerations include the fund's objective, expense ratio, and historical performance.

Examples of BTCETFs: ProShares Bitcoin Strategy ETF (BITO) and ProShares Short Bitcoin ETF (BITI).

4. Brokerage Interface: Log in to the brokerage account and navigate the platform's interface. Look for the search or trading section where you can find information about BTCETFs.

5. Ticker Symbol: Each BTCETFs has a unique ticker symbol. You(Investors) can search for the desired BTCETFs using its ticker symbol within the brokerage interface.

Example:(BITO, BITI, XBTF).

6. Quantity and Order: Enter the number of shares you want to purchase and specify any other relevant parameters, such as

order type (market or limit). Once you're satisfied, proceed to place the buy order.

7. Confirmation and Settlement: After placing the order for your desired BTCETFs, you'll receive a confirmation, and the trade settles. Settlement times can vary, but the purchased BTCETFs shares will eventually appear in your account.

Selling BTCETFs:

1. Log In to Brokerage Account: To sell BTCETFs shares, log in to the brokerage account using the provided credentials. Example, username or passwords.

2. Navigate to Portfolio or Trading Section: Locate the portfolio or trading section on the brokerage platform where you can view your holdings and execute sell orders.

3. BTCETF to Sell: Choose the specific BTCETFs shares you wish to sell from your portfolio.

4. Quantity and Sell Order: Enter the quantity of BTCETFs shares you want to sell and provide any additional details, such as order type. Proceed to place the sell order.

5. Confirmation and Settlement: Following the sell order, investors receive a confirmation. The settlement process begins, and the proceeds from the sale become available in the investor's account.

6. Review and Analyze: After selling, you(investor) may want to review the transaction and analyze the overall performance. This assessment can inform future investment decisions.

Keynote:

It's crucial for investors to stay informed about market conditions, monitor their portfolios regularly, and consider factors like expense ratios and associated costs when engaging in the buying and selling process of BTCETFs as well as other assets and ETFs in the financial market.

How to Choosing the Right BTCETFs

Selecting the right Bitcoin Exchange Traded Funds (BTCETFs) requires careful consideration of various factors to align with investment goals and risk tolerance of the investors.

Here is a guide on key aspects to evaluate when making this crucial decision:

1. Assets Under Management (AUM):
* Assess the Assets Under Management (AUM) of the BTCETFs. A higher AUM often indicates greater investor confidence and market acceptance.
* Consider the fund's growth trajectory and whether the AUM aligns with your expectations for liquidity and stability.

2. SEC Approval and Regulatory Status:
* Investigate the Securities and Exchange Commission (SEC) approval status of the BTCETFs. SEC approval lends credibility to the fund and ensures compliance with regulatory standards.

* Check if there have been any regulatory actions or concerns related to the specific BTCETFs, as this can impact its performance and legitimacy.

3. Year of Approval by Regulatory Bodies:
* Examine the year of approval by regulatory bodies, e.g, the SEC, the Financial Conduct Authority (FCA). A longer track record may provide insights into the BTCETF's performance through various market conditions.
* Consider how the BTCETFs has navigated regulatory changes and market challenges since its approval.

4. BTCETFs Entity or Managers:
* Evaluate the entity or management team behind the BTCETFs. Reputable and experienced entities inspire confidence in the fund's management.
* Research the track record and expertise of the fund managers. A skilled and knowledgeable management team is crucial for making sound investment decisions.

5. Expense Ratios and Fees:

* Scrutinize the expense ratios and fees associated with the BTCETFs. Lower expense ratios contribute to cost-effective investing and can have a positive impact on overall returns.

* Compare the fees of different BTCETFs to ensure that you are getting value for your investment.

6. Investment Objective and Strategy:

* Understand the investment objective and strategy of the BTCETFs. Different funds may have varying approaches, such as actively or passively managed strategies.

* Choose a BTCETFs whose investment approach aligns with your financial goals and risk appetite.

7. Liquidity and Trading Volume:

* Examine the liquidity and trading volume of the BTCETFs. Higher liquidity ensures that investors can buy or sell shares with ease, reducing the impact of bid-ask spreads.

* Adequate trading volume contributes to market efficiency and price stability.

8. Market Performance and Historical Data:

* Analyze the historical performance of the BTCETFs, considering factors like market trends, returns, and volatility.

* Review how the fund has performed during various market conditions to gauge its resilience and suitability for your investment strategy.

Keynote:

Choosing the right BTCETFs involves a comprehensive evaluation of these factors, ensuring that your investment aligns with your financial objectives and risk tolerance. Stay informed about market developments and regularly review your investment strategy to adapt accordingly to changing conditions.

Chapter 7

Comparing BTCETFs with Traditional Investments

Key Differences and Similarities with Traditional ETFs

Differences:

1. Underlying Asset:
   - BTCETFs: Track the real-time price of Bitcoin, a digital cryptocurrency.
   - Traditional ETFs: Track the performance of various assets or commodities, such as stocks, bonds, or commodities like gold.

2. Market Volatility:

- BTCETFs: Exhibit higher volatility due to the inherent nature of cryptocurrencies.
- Traditional ETFs: Generally experience lower volatility, influenced by the stability of the underlying assets.

3. Regulatory Environment:
- BTCETFs: Operate in a relatively nascent and evolving regulatory landscape, subject to specific challenges in approval and acceptance.
- Traditional ETFs: Operate within established regulatory frameworks, providing a more predictable environment for investors.

4. Asset Class Exposure:
- BTCETFs: Provide exposure to the cryptocurrency asset class, appealing to investors interested in digital assets.
- Traditional ETFs: Offer exposure to a diverse range of asset classes,

allowing investors to build diversified portfolios.

5. Technological Risks:
- BTCETFs: Face unique technological risks, including cybersecurity threats and the potential impact of blockchain technology developments.
- Traditional ETFs: Are less exposed to specific technological risks associated with blockchain or decentralized technologies.

Similarities:

1. Exchange-Traded Structure:
- BTCETFs: Share the same exchange-traded structure, allowing investors to buy and sell shares on stock exchanges during market hours.
- Traditional ETFs: Also trade on stock exchanges, providing investors with flexibility in trading.

2. Creation and Redemption Process:

- BTCETFs: Utilize the creation and redemption process involving authorized participants to manage the number of outstanding shares.
- Traditional ETFs: Employ a similar creation and redemption mechanism, enhancing liquidity and keeping the ETF's market price in line with its net asset value.

3. Expense Ratios:
- BTCETFs: Incur annual expense ratios, representing the cost of managing and operating the fund.
- Traditional ETFs: Also have expense ratios, covering management fees, administrative costs, and other operational expenses.

4. Investor Accessibility:
- BTCETFs: Offer accessibility to a broader range of investors, including those interested in the cryptocurrency market.
- Traditional ETFs: Cater to investors seeking exposure to traditional asset

classes, providing diverse investment opportunities.

5. Transparent Holdings Reporting:
- BTCETFs: Disclose holdings regularly, allowing investors to monitor the fund's composition and verify its alignment with the underlying Bitcoin market.
- Traditional ETFs: Maintain transparency by regularly disclosing their holdings, enhancing investor confidence and informed decision-making.

Keynote:

Understanding these key differences and similarities is essential for investors to make informed decisions based on their investment objectives, risk tolerance, and preferences. While both BTCETFs and traditional ETFs share certain characteristics, their distinctive features highlight the unique opportunities and challenges associated with each.

Market Impact and Investor Sentiment

Here is an exploration of market impact and investor sentiment in the financial markets:

Market Impact:

1. Price Movements:
* Market impact refers to the effect a specific event or news has on asset prices.
* Significant announcements, economic data releases, or geopolitical events can cause immediate and impactful price movements in various markets.

2. Liquidity Changes:
* Market impact often leads to shifts in liquidity.
* During times of heightened impact, liquidity may decrease as market participants reassess their positions and adjust to new information.

3. Volatility Fluctuations:

* Market impact influences volatility levels.
* Sudden events can result in increased volatility as traders react to new information, leading to larger price swings.

4. Order Book Dynamics:
* Large trades or market-moving events impact the order book.
* The order book may experience changes in depth and spread as traders adjust their positions in response to the market impact.

5. Trading Volumes:
* Market impact affects trading volumes.
* Increased market impact often corresponds with higher trading volumes as investors react to and execute trades based on the evolving market conditions.

Investor Sentiment:

1. Psychological Factors:
* Investor sentiment is influenced by psychological factors such as fear, greed, and market euphoria.

* Positive sentiment can lead to bullish market behavior, while negative sentiment may drive bearish trends.

2. News and Information Flow:
* Sentiment is shaped by the continuous flow of news and information.
* Positive or negative news can sway investor sentiment, impacting their outlook on specific assets or the overall market.

3. Social Media and Market Chatter:
* Social media platforms and online forums play a role in shaping investor sentiment.
* Market chatter and discussions on these platforms can contribute to the collective sentiment, influencing trading decisions.

4. Technical Analysis Signals:
* Technical analysis indicators, such as moving averages or chart patterns, can impact investor sentiment.
* Traders often use technical signals to gauge market sentiment and make informed trading decisions.

5. Economic Indicators:

* Economic indicators, such as employment reports or GDP growth, impact investor sentiment.
* Positive economic data can boost sentiment, while negative indicators may lead to a more cautious or pessimistic outlook.

Keynote:

Understanding both market impact and investor sentiment is crucial for navigating financial markets. Investors need to assess the potential impact of events on asset prices while also being attuned to the prevailing sentiment, as it can influence market trends and the decision-making of other market participants.

Chapter 8

Case Studies and Performance Analysis

Examining Historical Data of U.S Approved BTCETFs

The historical performance of six prominent BTCETFs (futures) that have gained approval mostly in the United States. These funds provide investors exposure to the dynamic world of Bitcoin, each with its unique strategy and approach. The outstanding BTCETFs as of the time of writing this book are:

1. ProShares Bitcoin Strategy ETF (BITO):
   - Overview: BITO aims to track the performance of Bitcoin futures contracts, offering investors a

straightforward way to gain exposure to Bitcoin's price movements.

- Performance Analysis: YTD Daily Total Return– 132.37%. 1-Year Daily Total Return– 127.36%.
  (These analyses are as a result of the explorations on how BITO has responded to various market conditions, assessing its returns, volatility, and correlation with the actual price of Bitcoin).

2. ProShares Short Bitcoin ETF (BITI):
- Overview: BITI takes a unique approach by seeking to provide short exposure to Bitcoin futures, allowing investors to potentially profit from declining Bitcoin prices.
- Performance Analysis: YTD Daily Total Return– -65.32%. 1-Year Daily Total Return– -64.81%.
  (These analyses result from an exploration on how BITI has performed during periods of Bitcoin price downturns and its effectiveness as a hedging tool.

3. VanEck Bitcoin Strategy ETF (XBTF):
- Overview: XBTF is designed to track the MVIS® CryptoCompare Bitcoin VWAP Close Index, providing exposure to Bitcoin's price movements.
- Performance Analysis: YTD Daily Total Return– 127.01%. 1-Year Daily Total Return– 122.95%.
  (These analyses result from an exploration of XBTF's historical performance, assessing its tracking accuracy and gauging the impact of market trends on its returns).

4. Valkyrie Bitcoin Strategy ETF (BTF):
- Overview: BTF seeks to achieve the performance of Bitcoin futures by utilizing a combination of long and short positions.
- Performance Analysis: YTD Daily Total Return– 128.88%. 1-Year Daily Total Return– 125.13%.
  (The results stem from an analysis of BTF's historical data, providing insights into how its strategy has performed in various market

scenarios and its efficacy in capturing Bitcoin price movements).

5. Simplify Bitcoin Strategy PLUS Inc ETF (MAXI):

- Overview: MAXI employs a systematic strategy to manage exposure to Bitcoin futures, aiming to enhance risk-adjusted returns.
- Performance Analysis: YTD Daily Total Return– 137.27%. 1-Year Daily Total Return– 133.96%.
  (The results are from an exploration of MAXI's historical data, examining how its systematic approach has influenced both its overall performance and risk management).

6. Global X Blockchain & Bitcoin Strategy ETF (BITS):

- Overview: BITS provides exposure to both Bitcoin and companies involved in blockchain technology, offering a diversified approach within the cryptocurrency space.

- Performance Analysis: YTD Daily Total Return– 165.37%. 1-Year Daily Total Return– 145.88%.
  (These results are derived from analyses of BITS's historical data, assessing how its dual exposure to Bitcoin and blockchain-related assets has impacted its overall performance).

Keynote:

By scrutinizing the historical performance of these six U.S approved BTCETFs, investors can gain valuable insights into their behavior, risk-return profiles, and effectiveness in delivering on their investment objectives. This examination provides a comprehensive view of how these funds have navigated the evolving cryptocurrency landscape, aiding investors in making informed decisions about their investment strategies.

Real-world Examples of BTCETFs and Total Assets

Here are real-world examples of some BTCETFs along with their total assets:

1. ETF Name: ProShares Bitcoin Strategy ETF (BITO).
   - Total Assets: $1,658.34(Please check the latest data for accurate figures).

2. ETF Name: ProShares Short Bitcoin ETF (BITI).
   - Total Assets: $65 billion(Please check the latest data for accurate figures.)

3. ETF Name: VanEck Bitcoin Strategy ETF (XBTF).
   - Total Assets: $70.14(Please check the latest data for accurate figures.)

4. ETF Name: Valkyrie Bitcoin Strategy ETF (BTF).
   - Total Assets: $38.93(Please check the latest data for accurate figures.)

5. ETF Name: Simplify Bitcoin Strategy PLUS Inc ETF (MAXI).
- Total Assets: (Please check the latest data for accurate figures.)

6. ETF Name: Global X Blockchain & Bitcoin Strategy ETF (BITS).
- Total Assets: $20.01(Please check the latest data for accurate figures.)

7. ETF Name: ARK Next Generation Internet ETF(ARKW)
- Total Assets: $1,605.54(Please check the latest data for accurate figures)

8. ETF Name: Bitwise Crypto Industry Innovators ETF(BITQ)
- Total Assets: $115.30(Please check the latest data for accurate figures)

9. ETF Name: Valkyrie Bitcoin Miners ETF(WGMI)
- Total Assets: $33.82(Please check the latest data for accurate figures).

10. ETF Name: Bitwise Bitcoin and Ether Equal Weight Strategy ETF(BTOP)

- Total Assets: $3.72(Please check the latest data for accurate figures)

Keynote:

Have it in mind that specific total assets may change over time; for real-time and accurate information on the total assets of each BTCETFs, it's advisable to refer to reputable financial sources or the official websites of the respective ETFs.

Chapter 9

The Future Outlook and Emerging Trends

Future Predictions for BTCETFs

Drawing insights from both historical and current price trends of Bitcoin ETFs, coupled with an analysis of Bitcoin halving cycles, we project the anticipated yearly low and high price predictions for the upcoming year, 2024. The forecast places the estimated yearly low for Bitcoin ETFs at $0.000190 and envisions the potential for prices to surge to as high as $0.000503.

Expanding on this methodology, we extend our Bitcoin ETFs price predictions for the subsequent years, from 2024 through 2030, employing the same analytical foundation to provide a comprehensive outlook on the potential price movements of these ETFs over the specified timeframe. Here is the list of our predictions:

Year	Yearly Low	Yearly High
2024	$ 0.000190	$ 0.000503
2025	$ 0.000425	$ 0.001716
2026	$ 0.000473	$ 0.000785
2027	$ 0.000497	$ 0.001232
2028	$ 0.001073	$ 0.001213
2029	$ 0.001158	$ 0.002183
2030	$ 0.001234	$ 0.001561

Keynote: we anticipate and project the yearly low and high price predictions for Bitcoin ETFs in 2024, based on historical and present price movements as well as considerations of BTC halving cycles. The estimated range spans from $0.000190 for the yearly low in 2024 to a potential high of $0.001561 in 2030.

These projections aim to assist investors in making informed decisions and provide insights into the potential trajectory of Bitcoin ETFs in the financial market(Please note that these predictions solely represent the views of the writers, and the accuracy of these predictions is uncertain).

Future Predictions for Bitcoin/BTCETFs Spot after SEC's Approval

Cryptocurrency services provider Matrix Port envisions a potential surge in Bitcoin's value to $56,000 following SEC approval of a spot Bitcoin ETF. Their report suggests a conservative estimate of Bitcoin reaching $42,000, driven by 10-20% of gold ETF investors diversifying into Bitcoin.

With over $200 billion invested in gold ETFs, even a 10% shift could inject $12-24 billion into a Bitcoin ETF, comparable to the assets under management of the Grayscale Bitcoin Trust at its peak.

Matrix Port further highlights the untapped potential of the 15,000 registered investment advisors overseeing $5 trillion in assets, projecting a $50 billion inflow into Bitcoin with a modest 1% Bitcoin allocation recommendation (according to Matrix Port).

Fundstrat's head of research, Tom Lee, offers an even more optimistic outlook, suggesting Bitcoin could skyrocket to over

$150,000 by the end of 2024 if multiple spot Bitcoin ETFs gain approval in the US. Lee emphasizes the potential for ETF demand to outpace Bitcoin's daily supply, potentially driving the price as high as $180,000. Noting that Europe already has spot Bitcoin ETFs in play, Lee underscores the outsized impact that US-approved ETFs could have on Bitcoin's price (according to Tom Lee).

Ernst & Young's global blockchain leader, Paul Brody, underscores the significant pent-up demand from institutional investors awaiting SEC approval of a spot Bitcoin ETF. Brody believes trillions of institutional dollars are poised to enter the Bitcoin market once regulatory barriers are removed.

In a recent CNBC interview, he highlighted that institutions view Bitcoin as an investment asset, and once they can access it through an ETF, a substantial influx of institutional capital is anticipated to drive up Bitcoin's price significantly (according to Paul Brody).

While not providing a precise prediction, EY's analysis adds another bullish perspective, emphasizing the potential flood of institutional demand upon ETF approval (according to Ernst & Young).

Keynote:

These predictions from various experts collectively paint a promising future for Bitcoin and BTCETFs after SEC approval. The potential influx of institutional capital, coupled with increased demand driven by ETFs, could propel Bitcoin's value to new heights, reshaping the cryptocurrency landscape in the coming years.

Chapter 10

FAQs and Glossary.

Frequently Asked Questions And Answers

Here are some potential frequently asked questions (FAQs) with corresponding answers covering common queries from beginners, investors, and crypto enthusiasts:

1. Q: What is cryptocurrency?
A: Cryptocurrency is a digital or virtual form of currency that uses cryptography for security and operates on decentralized networks, typically based on blockchain technology.

2. Q: How do I buy my first cryptocurrency?
A: You can buy cryptocurrency on various online platforms known as exchanges, eg,

Binance, Okx, Bybit, etc. Create an account, deposit funds, and choose the cryptocurrency you wish to purchase.

3. Q: What is a wallet, and why do I need one?
A: A wallet is a digital tool that allows you to store, send, and receive cryptocurrencies. It's essential for securely managing your crypto assets.
Example, Trust wallet, Metamask wallet, etc.

4. Q: Are cryptocurrencies legal?
A: Cryptocurrency legality varies by country. In many places, they are legal, but it's crucial to understand and comply with your local regulations.

5. Q: How can I keep my cryptocurrencies safe?
A: Use secure wallets, enable two-factor authentication, and store backup phrases offline(usually 12 sets of different words). Be cautious of phishing scams and only use reputable exchanges.

6. Q: What factors influence the price of cryptocurrencies?
A: Cryptocurrency prices are influenced by factors such as market demand, supply, regulatory developments, technological advancements, and macroeconomic trends.

7. Q: How do I diversify my cryptocurrency portfolio?
A: Diversify by investing in different cryptocurrencies and industry sectors. Avoid putting all your funds into a single asset to reduce risk.

8. Q: What is the significance of market capitalization?
A: Market capitalization represents the total value of a cryptocurrency. It's calculated by multiplying the current price by the total circulating supply and reflects the market's perception of its worth.

9. Q: Should I invest in initial coin offerings (ICOs)?
A: ICOs come with higher risks. Before investing, thoroughly research the project, its team, and whitepaper. Many

investors/traders prefer to wait until a project has a more established track record.

10. Q: How do taxes work with cryptocurrency investments?
A: Tax regulations vary by jurisdiction. Keep records of your transactions, report capital gains, and consider consulting a tax professional for accurate advice.

11. Q: What is decentralized finance (DeFi)?
A: DeFi refers to decentralized financial services built on blockchain technology, offering alternatives to traditional banking and financial systems.

12. Q: How can I participate in staking?
A: Staking involves actively participating in transaction validation on a proof-of-stake (PoS) blockchain. Research and choose a PoS project, lock up your tokens, and earn rewards(optional).

13. Q: What is a non-fungible token (NFT)?
A: NFTs are digital(unique) assets, mostly representing ownership of physical or digital items. They use blockchain

technology to certify authenticity and uniqueness.

14. Q: How does yield farming work?
A: Yield farming involves lending or staking cryptocurrencies in decentralized finance protocols to earn interest or additional tokens as rewards.

15. Q: Can you explain the concept of decentralized autonomous organizations (DAOs)?
A: DAOs are organizations run by code, allowing members to make decisions collectively. Voting power is often proportionate to the number of tokens held.

16. Q: How do I choose the right cryptocurrency exchange?
A: Consider factors like security features, fees, available cryptocurrencies, user interface, and customer support when selecting a cryptocurrency exchange(watch out for our new release on top cryptocurrency to buy for maximum profit).

17. Q: Can I lose more money than I invest in cryptocurrencies?
A: No, your losses are limited to the amount you invest. However, market fluctuations can impact your investment's value.

18. Q: What is the difference between a hot wallet and a cold wallet?
A: A hot wallet is connected to the internet and is suitable for regular transactions, while a cold wallet is offline and provides enhanced security for long-term storage.

19. Q: Is it too late to invest in Bitcoin?
A: Bitcoin remains a viable investment. Consider your goals, risk tolerance, and do your research before deciding to invest or consult a certified financial advisor for more information.

20. Q: How do I sell my cryptocurrencies and convert them to fiat currency?
A: You can sell your cryptocurrencies on an exchange, and then withdraw the funds to your linked bank account.

21. Q: What is dollar-cost averaging (DCA), and how can it benefit me?

A: DCA involves regularly investing a fixed amount, regardless of market conditions. It helps reduce the impact of market volatility on your investment.

22. Q: Can I invest in cryptocurrencies through my retirement account?

A: Yes, some retirement accounts offer options for investing in cryptocurrencies. Consult with your financial advisor for guidance.

23. Q: How can I stay updated on cryptocurrency market trends?

A: Follow reputable news sources, join online communities, and regularly review market data on cryptocurrency tracking platforms.

Example: Trading view, coinmarketcap, Coingecko, etc.

24. Q: What is the significance of whitepapers in cryptocurrency projects?

A: Whitepapers provide detailed information about a cryptocurrency project, including its technology, goals, and how it plans to solve existing challenges.

25. Q: Are there any risks associated with using leverage in cryptocurrency trading?
A: Yes, leverage amplifies both gains and losses. Use it cautiously, understanding the risks involved, and only with funds you can afford to lose.

26. Q: How does liquidity impact cryptocurrency trading?
A: Higher liquidity typically leads to narrower bid-ask spreads, making it easier to execute trades at desired prices.

27. Q: What is a decentralized exchange (DEX)?
A: A DEX is a cryptocurrency exchange that operates without a central authority, allowing users to trade directly from their wallets.
Example: Uniswap, Kyber, PancakeSwap, etc.

28. Q: Can I use cryptocurrencies for everyday purchases?

A: Some merchants accept cryptocurrencies as payment. However, widespread adoption for everyday transactions is still evolving.

29. Q: How does cross-border remittance work with cryptocurrencies?
A: Cryptocurrencies enable faster and potentially more cost-effective cross-border transfers compared to traditional banking systems.

30. Q: What are the potential environmental concerns associated with cryptocurrency mining?
A: Cryptocurrency mining, particularly for Proof-of-Work (PoW) coins, has raised concerns due to its energy consumption. Some projects are exploring more energy-efficient alternatives.

31. Q: What is an ETF, and how does it differ from traditional stocks?
A: An ETF, also known as an Exchange-Traded Fund, is a form of investment vehicle that owns a diverse portfolio of assets. It trades on an exchange,

similar to a stock, providing investors with exposure to various assets.

32. Q: How do I buy BTCETFs?
A: Buying BTCETFs is similar to buying stocks. You can do so through a brokerage account. Search for the BTCETFs ticker symbol on your broker's platform, specify the quantity, and place your order.

33. Q: Are BTCETFs safer than individual cryptocurrencies?
A: BTCETFs can offer a more diversified and less volatile(risk) exposure to cryptocurrencies compared to individual tokens. However, they still carry market risks.

34. Q: What is the expense ratio in an ETF?
A: The expense ratio is the annual fee expressed as a percentage of an ETF's average net assets. It covers operational costs and management fees.

35. Q: Can I trade BTCETFs like stocks throughout the day?

A: Yes, BTCETFs, like traditional ETFs, are traded on stock exchanges and can be bought or sold throughout the trading day at market prices.

36. Q: How do I analyze the performance of a BTCETFs?
A: Evaluate historical performance, expense ratios, tracking error, and the underlying assets to analyze a BTCETF's performance.

37. Q: What is the role of an Authorized Participant (AP) in the creation/redemption process of BTCETFs?
A: APs play a crucial role in creating and redeeming ETF shares. They help maintain the balance between the ETF's market price and its net asset value (NAV).

38. Q: Are BTCETFs subject to capital gains taxes?
A: Yes, selling BTC ETF shares may result in capital gains taxes. Because the tax effects might differ, it is best to contact a tax specialist.

39. Q: How are dividends handled in BTCETFs?
A: Some BTCETFs may distribute dividends, while others reinvest them. Check the ETF's prospectus to understand its dividend distribution policy.

40. Q: Can I use BTCETFs for long-term investing?
A: Yes, BTCETFs can be part of a long-term investment strategy. Evaluate your financial goals and risk tolerance before incorporating them into your portfolio.

41. Q: How do BTCETFs track the price of Bitcoin?
A: BTCETFs typically use various strategies, such as holding physical Bitcoin, Bitcoin futures, or a combination, to track the price of Bitcoin.

42. Q: What impact can regulatory developments have on BTCETFs?
A: Regulatory changes can significantly affect BTCETFs. Approval or disapproval of ETF applications by regulatory bodies can influence their performance.

43. Q: Are there leveraged or inverse BTCETFs?

A: Yes, some ETFs offer leveraged or inverse exposure to Bitcoin price movements. However, these come with increased risk and are suitable for experienced investors.

44. Q: How does the creation and redemption process affect BTC ETF prices?

A: The creation and redemption process helps keep BTC ETF prices in line with the net asset value (NAV), ensuring efficient trading on the exchange.

45. Q: Can BTCETFs be used as a hedge against market volatility?

A: Yes, BTCETFs can provide a diversified and liquid asset, potentially serving as a hedge against market volatility. However, their effectiveness depends on various factors.

46. Q: How do BTCETFs differ from traditional Bitcoin exchanges?

A: BTCETFs provide a way to gain exposure to Bitcoin without directly owning and managing the cryptocurrency. They are traded on stock exchanges, offering a more accessible and regulated investment avenue.

47. Q: Can I reinvest dividends from BTCETFs automatically?

A: Many BTCETFs offer dividend reinvestment programs (DRIPs), allowing investors to automatically reinvest dividends to acquire additional shares.

48. Q: What role do market makers play in the liquidity of BTCETFs?

A: Market makers facilitate liquidity by buying and selling ETF shares, helping to maintain price stability and ensure efficient trading on the exchange.

Keynote:

The above FAQs have "Q" for Questions and "A" for Answers.

Always seek professional financial advice and conduct thorough research before making investment decisions. Information provided here is for educational purposes only.

Glossary of key terms in Cryptocurrency and ETFs financial market.

Here are some key terms arranged in alphabetical order for both Cryptocurrency and ETFs financial markets:

Cryptocurrency Glossary:

1. Altcoin:Any cryptocurrency other than Bitcoin.

2. Blockchain: A decentralized, distributed ledger technology that records transactions across a network of computers.

3. Cold Wallet: A secure offline storage solution for cryptocurrency.

4. Decentralized Finance (DeFi): Financial services built on blockchain technology, offering alternatives to traditional banking.

5. Exchange: An online platform where users can buy, sell, and trade cryptocurrencies.

6. Fiat Currency: Traditional government-issued currency, such as the US Dollar or Euro.

7. Hash Rate: The speed at which a computer can perform operations in the cryptocurrency network.

8. ICO (Initial Coin Offering): A fundraising method where new projects sell their underlying cryptocurrency tokens to early investors.

9. Mining: The process of validating transactions and adding them to the

blockchain, typically involving solving complex mathematical problems.

10. Node: A computer on the blockchain network that maintains a copy of the entire blockchain.

11. Orphan Block: A valid block that is not part of the main blockchain.

12. Private Key: A secret cryptographic key that allows access to one's cryptocurrency.

13. QR Code: A two-dimensional barcode used to store information, often used in cryptocurrency wallets.

14. Smart Contract: Self-executing contracts with the terms of the agreement directly written into code.

15. Token: A digital asset created on a blockchain that represents ownership of a real or digital asset.

ETFs Glossary:

16. Authorized Participant (AP): A participant, usually a large institution, that can create or redeem shares of an ETF.

17. Bear Market: A market characterized by declining prices and pessimism.

18. Creation Unit: The block of shares an ETF issuer assembles to form an ETF.

19. Dividend Yield: The annual dividend income an ETF pays relative to its share price.

20. Expense Ratio: The annual fee expressed as a percentage of an ETF's average net assets.

21. Index: A benchmark that an ETF aims to replicate or outperform.

22. Liquidity: The ease with which an ETF can be bought or sold on the market.

23. Management Fee: The fee paid to the investment manager for managing the ETF.

24. Net Asset Value (NAV): The total value of an ETF's assets minus its liabilities.

25. Open-End Fund: An ETF that continuously issues and redeems shares based on investor demand.

26. Premium/Discount: The difference between an ETF's market price and its NAV.

27. Rebalancing: Adjusting the holdings of an ETF to maintain its target asset allocation.

28. Sector ETF: An ETF that invests in companies within a specific sector of the economy.

29. Tracking Error: The divergence between the performance of an ETF and its benchmark.

30. Yield: The income generated by an ETF's holdings, often expressed as a percentage.

Keynote:

This glossary provides brief definitions for each term. For a comprehensive understanding, you can further research and consult with financial professionals(recommended).

<u>BONUS</u>

Three Cryptos With 10X Potential You should Buy As Soon As Possible

BITCOIN(BTC)

Many believe that the blue-chip of cryptocurrencies can potentially trade above $400,000 by 2027.

Let's explore some reasons to be bullish on Bitcoin.

The halving event is projected to be a key catalyst in 2024. In the past, Bitcoin halving has been followed by a spectacular surge. According to Standard Chartered, Bitcoin will be worth $120,000 by the end of 2024, representing a threefold increase from current prices.

Another significant imminent trigger for Bitcoin is the possibility of a spot ETF. Analysts anticipate it will arrive in early 2024, causing significant purchasing. Furthermore, global economic trends suggest that interest rates may be decreased next year. Bitcoin is anticipated to do well during periods of expansionary monetary policy.

Finally, the demand-supply dynamic is likely to be at work. As cryptocurrency acceptance grows internationally, Bitcoin is expected to rise due to strong demand and limited supply. As a result, it is not unreasonable to predict that Bitcoin is one of the cryptocurrency with 10X potential.

UNISWAP (UNI)

Franklin Templeton CEO Jenny Johnson has recently revealed that she owns Bitcoin, Ethereum (ETH-USD), Uniswap (UNI-USD), and Sushi (SUSHI-USD) in her portfolio. Positions taken by major investors boost trust and confidence in cryptocurrencies.

It's reasonable to be optimistic about Uniswap's long-term prospects. As an overview, Uniswap is a decentralized exchange. In terms of trade volume, it is the world's largest decentralized exchange.

In May 2021, the UNI token was worth around $45. Even if the token touches previous all-time highs, it would imply almost 8x returns from current levels of $6. Given Bitcoin's projected growth, 10x would be a simple aim for UNI token. Trading volumes (both centralized and decentralized) will increase as cryptocurrencies rise in value. This is likely to benefit Uniswap.

Regulations that apply equally to centralized and decentralized exchanges pose a challenge to the optimistic thesis for Uniswap. Even with that feature, Uniswap is appealing due to the continued rise in total value locked.

ZILLIQA (ZIL)

Zilliqa (ZIL-USD) is another coin where 10x
or 20x returns are a likelihood. During my
observation of the last bull market, ZIL coin
reached highs of 25 cents. Even if those
highs are re-tested, ZIL would return 11x.
This scenario is quite likely to play out
sooner than planned.

The Zilliqa network claims to be the world's
first network to use the sharding idea.
Transactions are broken into smaller

chunks and distributed across miners for parallel transaction verification. The result is a swift transaction. Furthermore, Zilliqa is substantially less expensive than Bitcoin or Ethereum.

Aside from this essential aspect, ZIL coin features an appealing staking incentive. The current APR is 13.18%(As of the time of writing this book). For an undervalued coin, the attractive APR is a significant benefit. As the cryptocurrency world grows, so will the number of dApps on Zilliqa. Therefore, ZIL is likely to see strong demand.

Keynote:

The views presented above are solely those of the writer, and neither the writer nor any affiliated parties hold any positions (either directly or indirectly) in the securities mentioned herein. It is important to clarify that the information provided docs not constitute financial advice. Individuals are strongly advised to conduct thorough research and seek guidance from certified financial advisors before making any final decisions.

Feel free to leave your view, predictions or speculations about these cryptos on the review page of this guide.

Recap of Key Takeaways

1. Bitcoin ETF Evolution: Bitcoin ETFs mark a pivotal convergence of cryptocurrency and traditional finance.
Regulatory hurdles delayed approval until October 2021, signaling a transformative shift.

2. BTC-ETF Basics: BTC-ETFs offer exposure to bitcoin's price movements without holding the asset directly.
Tradable on traditional stock exchanges, making them accessible to mainstream investors.

3. ETFs in Financial Markets: ETFs are recognized as both investment products and vehicles in financial markets.
They encompass various structures, including index funds and sector-specific ETFs.

4. Types of Bitcoin ETFs: Spot Bitcoin ETFs hold actual bitcoin, tracking real-time prices closely.

Futures Bitcoin ETFs use contracts, offering different exposure with potential leverage.

5. Regulatory Considerations: Regulatory concerns included market manipulation, liquidity, and investor protection.
Approval of ProShares Bitcoin Strategy ETF opened regulated entry for institutional and retail investors.

6. Market Impact and Acceptance: Green light for Bitcoin ETFs in the U.S. reflects increasing acceptance within mainstream financial markets.
Signals a shift in perception and showcases the evolving landscape of cryptocurrencies.

7. BTCETFs Approval: The approval of Bitcoin ETFs(futures) represents a significant chapter in the evolving narrative of digital assets.
Mainstream acceptance, regulatory clarity, and diverse investment options contribute to the growing importance of BTC-ETFs in the financial landscape.

8. Future Predictions and Expert Views: Expert insights suggest potential surges in Bitcoin's price with SEC approval of spot Bitcoin ETFs.

Predictions include price trajectories from 2024 to 2030 based on historical and current trends.

9. Investment Considerations: BTC-ETFs serve as regulated entry points for investors to engage with the cryptocurrency market.

Investors advised to conduct thorough research, consider risk tolerance, and consult financial professionals.

10. Cryptocurrency and ETFs Glossary: Familiarize yourself with key terms in both cryptocurrency and ETFs for a comprehensive understanding.

CONCLUSION

In our extensive exploration of Bitcoin Exchange-Traded Funds (BTC-ETFs) and related topics, you've witnessed a groundbreaking chapter unfold in the convergence of cryptocurrency and traditional finance. From the challenges of regulatory approval to the distinct characteristics of Spot and Futures Bitcoin ETFs, each facet contributes to the evolving narrative of digital assets in mainstream markets.

Understanding the distinctions between Spot and Futures ETFs, regulatory considerations, and market dynamics will empower you to make informed decisions.

The approval of BTC-ETFs futures, particularly in the U.S, signifies a transformative shift, reflecting growing acceptance within the financial mainstream. As these financial instruments become increasingly integral, the need for investors and enthusiasts to grasp their nuances becomes imperative.

For investors entering the cryptocurrency space through BTC-ETFs, our key notes and takeaways emphasize the importance of thorough research, considering risk tolerance, and seeking advice from certified financial professionals.

As you navigate the exciting yet dynamic world of cryptocurrency investments linked with its financial products, we wish you strategic insights, profitable ventures, and the resilience to adapt to market shifts. May your financial journey be marked by success, guided by knowledge, and enriched with the thrill of participating in the transformative landscape of digital assets.

May your financial future be filled with prosperity and opportunities!

Happy Investing!!!

Dear Esteemed Reader, I invite you to share your insights about this financial handbook. Your feedback is invaluable in shaping the future editions and helping us serve you better. Kindly take a moment to provide your thoughts, and nice suggestions(write it along if you need access to our telegram community – we'll make it available in our next project). Your input is crucial, and we appreciate your time and dedication to enhancing this financial resource.

Best regards, Joel B. Albert